PUMP UP
THE VOLUME

PUMP UP THE VOLUME

Making the Oral Vocabulary Connection

by Laureen Reynolds

Crystal Springs
BOOKS

A division of SDE Staff Development for EDUCATORS

Peterborough, New Hampshire

Published by Crystal Springs Books
A division of Staff Development for Educators (SDE)
10 Sharon Road, PO Box 500
Peterborough, NH 03458
1-800-321-0401
www.crystalsprings.com

www.sde.com

Published 2008
Printed in the United States of America

12   11   10   09   08   1   2   3   4   5

ISBN: 978-1-934026-17-5

Library of Congress Cataloging-in-Publication Data

Reynolds, Laureen, 1969-

  Pump up the volume : making the oral vocabulary connection / by Laureen Reynolds.

     p. cm.

  "K-3."

  Includes bibliographical references and index.

  ISBN 978-1-934026-17-5

  1. Vocabulary--Study and teaching (Early childhood)--Activity programs. 2. Language arts (Early
childhood)--Activity programs. 3. Verbal ability in children. I. Title. II. Title: K-3 pump up the volume.

  LB1139.5.L35R49 2008

  372.44--dc22

                       2008038069

Editor: Sandra J. Taylor
Art Director and Designer: Soosen Dunholter
Production Coordinator: Deborah Fredericks
Illustrator: Joyce Rainville

Contents

Introduction

Words have played an important part in my life from the time my memories begin. I recall watching my father work the *New York Times* crossword puzzle in ink each Sunday afternoon. I am still in awe when I visit him, for he is a true wordsmith. We smile when he plays along with me, pretending he doesn't know some of the answers. My mother, always encouraging her children to do anything creative, got me started writing. She bought me books about words and used sophisticated vocabulary when she spoke to me.

I've been using words to write stories and poems since the second grade. I truly love words. But it was not until freshman year of high school that my ears became really aware of complex words like *anachronism* and *adroit* (even though they were presented in the traditional list-and-define format). After graduating from college, I was given my first opportunity to use words to affect a new generation in a classroom of my very own. Who knew the weight my spoken words would carry there?

As I look back, I wonder where I would be without words. Words have served as my foundation for reading about, writing for, speaking in, and listening to this world of ours. The spoken word is the starting point for nearly everything your students will set out to do, both now and in the future. It is the strength that every child possesses, whether she is an English language learner, a child from an impoverished background, or a mainstream American student. It's up to us as educators to help our students build the same foundation by talking to them and encouraging them to talk to us and to each other.

If you have a passion for speaking and hearing fine words, your students will too. As they develop their oral—listening and speaking—vocabularies, students aren't limited by their ability to read or write. If they can say a word and understand it, they can use it every day. Make them aware of how fabulous words can be and they will surprise you with something fabulous right back. And it is at *that* moment, when a

child comes to you with the most interesting word in the world, one he heard in conversation and then used himself, that you will know you've succeeded. But don't stop there. A mental warehouse of strong words they can use and understand will serve your students forever. Choose them carefully, shed light upon them frequently, and speak them often. Make magic with words.

Oral Vocabulary Basics

What are the best teaching methods for building our students' listening and speaking vocabularies? Which words should we teach? Can sophisticated oral vocabulary be taught before children can read or write? These are just a few of the questions that have surrounded vocabulary instruction and sparked debate among educators for many years. You may have the same questions (and more!) yourself. Fear not—the research tidbits below will help you unfurl, untangle, and understand just what teaching listening and speaking vocabulary should look and sound like.

◎ No consistent formula exists for determining "grade level" words. The only considerations when teaching a word to enhance a child's listening and speaking vocabularies should be: Can I explain it in words my students already know? Is this word going to be useful and interesting to them? (Beck, McKeown, and Kucan, 2002)

◎ The most important words to teach directly are words that students will encounter in many contexts—oral (for now) and written (later on). If a word is too topic specific, for example, oviparous (egg-laying), it should be explained only if it is encountered in a read-aloud. Children are not likely to hear or use that word often in conversation. (Beck, McKeown, and Kucan, 2002)

◎ Context clues are often insufficient for young readers, especially if they do not have the benefit of a strong oral vocabulary. (Beck, McKeown, and Kucan, 2002)

◎ Listening and speaking vocabulary instruction before grade three is most crucial—especially for children who come from less literate homes. After grade three, oral vocabulary acquisition happens at about the same rate for all learners. (Baumann and Kame'enui, 2004)

◎ Dictionary definitions should not be the first line of vocabulary instruction. They are often unclear, incomplete, and overwhelming. (Blachowicz and Fisher, 2006)

- Picture books, read aloud, should be a primary source of oral vocabulary introduction and expansion. There are more rare words per thousand in quality children's books than there are on television shows or in adult-to-adult conversation. (Trelease, 2001)

- Nonreaders and young readers learn most of their vocabulary through oral context and in conversations with peers and adults. (Beck, McKeown, and Kucan, 2002)

- Environmental print can be a vital piece of primary oral vocabulary instruction when the educator not only places the words around the room but also, more important, says them with frequency. (Blachowicz and Fisher, 2006)

- Elementary educators should be rereading books to their students as many as six times to strengthen and extend listening and speaking vocabulary acquisition. (Baumann and Kame'enui, 2004)

- Sophisticated vocabulary acquisition is not a passive activity. Children should have extensive, repeated, varied, and personal interactions with words we desire to add to their listening and speaking vocabularies. (Paynter, Bodrova, and Doty, 2005)

- Wide oral reading by a more literate other is crucial to a child's oral vocabulary acquisition and ownership. (Baumann and Kame'enui, 2004)

- Helping students to develop "word consciousness" (a curiosity about and awareness of interesting words) should be part of oral vocabulary instruction. (Beck, McKeown, and Kucan, 2002)

- The size of the oral vocabulary that a learner brings to the task of reading has a great impact on her comprehension as she develops as an independent reader. (Report of the National Reading Panel, 2000)

As primary teachers we spend a lot of time teaching students the simple words they can add to their early reading and writing vocabularies, but we spend very little time teaching to their oral strengths. We need to teach them words that will increase their listening and speaking vocabularies (words they understand when they hear them and use when they speak). These oral vocabularies are neglected at the cost of high-quality conversation, increased listening comprehension, and, later on, writing acumen and reading comprehension. If this sounds overwhelming, don't worry—the activities and strategies on the pages that follow will tell you exactly how to make it all happen.

Good Morning!

The most effective way to build oral vocabulary is to start with the known, and what better way than during your morning routine? Morning meeting is an important time in a primary classroom. Children greet each other, learn what the day will bring, and converse about important events in their personal lives. Incorporating sophisticated, useful, and interesting vocabulary during morning meeting will enhance its value even more. Start with your morning message. For example, you might write and say:

Welcome *Scholars*!

Today is Wednesday.

We'll be *congregating* in the gym this morning for a *unique* assembly about owls.

How many *species* of owls do you think exist?

Later on, we'll be *persistent* about finishing our field-trip stories.

When students read the message to themselves or listen as it is read to them, they will want to know about these words. Explain each word only briefly at first—enough to provide understanding in the context of the message. Then call attention to these words as many times as you can during the course of the day by using them in conversations, pointing them out in stories, and having your students listen for them in the hallway or lunchroom.

You can also bring unusual vocabulary to your greetings by teaching children different ways of saying hello, whether in another language or a more (or less) sophisticated English version. Here are a few suggestions:

Salutations	**Ciao**
Howdy	**Shalom**
Greetings	**Bonjour**
G'day	**Buenos Dias**

We can also stretch our students' oral vocabularies by renaming familiar morning meeting activities, such as *sharing* (which is a verbal version of the traditional Show and Tell). Once students know this label, you can begin to call it something else like *narrating*. If you do a physical exercise as part of your daily meeting, you might start calling it *calisthenics*.

Bring in the Books

Picture books serve as the introduction and extension for many of the concepts we teach. They are one of the most important tools in your listening and speaking—or oral—vocabulary instruction. Quality children's literature contains wonderful words that young readers are unlikely to encounter in other areas of their lives.

Making Choices

Instructional time in the classroom is precious, so when you are choosing read-alouds make sure they can serve more than one purpose. For example, Stuart Murphy's book *Tally O'Malley* introduces the concept of counting with tally marks, but it also includes oral vocabulary candidates, like *bundle*, *shamrock*, and *distance*, and conversations about colors. Remember, vocabulary instruction should not be limited to your language arts time. Oral vocabulary learning happens all day, every day—each time you speak or listen to each other.

Choose books that will offer opportunities for discussions, predictions, connections, and challenges. Also share books whose topic or main idea may be new to your students—expanding their vocabularies even more. See I Hear an Idea on page 30 for books with few or simple words, but whose concepts are ripe for the picking.

Try to choose books that your students are not likely to have heard in previous grades or at home. By first or second grade, many children are so familiar with the more well-known titles that their potential for new learning is reduced.

Picture Walks

We've all done these in reading groups somewhere along the way, but perhaps never realized the importance of picture walks for whole-group read-alouds and oral vocabulary growth. The conversations, questions, and answers that can ensue from looking at pictures with your class are a tremendous vocabulary opportunity just waiting to happen. Taking the extra time to do this with your favorite read-alouds will be priceless. Remember, children learn most of their vocabulary through oral context. Talking with them about what they are about to see and hear will increase not only their listening and speaking vocabularies but also their listening comprehension.

While there is no prescribed sequence for executing an effective picture walk, here are some things to keep in mind:

◎ Read the title and author of the book.

◎ Comment on the cover illustrations.

◎ Ask students to make some predictions based on information on the cover.

◎ Have your oral vocabulary candidates already selected, mark the pages where those words appear, and be sure to insert that vocabulary when appropriate during your picture walk.

◎ Make personal connections to the book and allow students to make some as well.

◎ Don't worry about addressing every page—it's not necessary.

◎ Keep the picture walk brief, light, and conversational.

Wide Reading

Providing a variety of reading materials (curriculum based as well as magazines, brochures, advertisements, and more) at a variety of reading levels will also increase vocabulary acquisition. Creating an environment that is flooded with printed text and pictures will facilitate vocabulary development indirectly, encourage that all-important conversation piece, and increase your students' interest in particular topics and reading in general. Even if your students are nonreaders, they have tremendous abilities to converse with peers about pictures they see in books and even connected personal experiences.

Pass on Your Passion

By using picture books as part of your listening and speaking vocabulary instruction, you are modeling a love of words for your students. Students develop "word consciousness" and "ownership" (Beck, McKeown, and Kucan, 2002) when the literate adults in their lives draw attention to interesting words. Children's literature is the best, most appropriate place to find those words and the most natural vehicle for discussion and extension.

Vocabulary Suggestions from Picture Books

Title	Author	Vocabulary
A Busy Year	Leo Lionni	blossoms, careless, unrolled
Apples to Oregon	Deborah Hopkinson and Nancy Carpenter	cozy, sneaking
Barfburger Baby, I Was Here First	Paula Danziger	annoying, cloth, drooling
Brave Irene	William Steig	clasped, errand, fret
Chameleons Are Cool	Martin Jenkins	peering, exhausted
If You Decide to Go to the Moon	Faith McNulty	horizon, rim, jagged, pebble
Mighty Jackie the Strike-Out Queen	Marissa Moss	glared, delicate, stunned
Mr. George Baker	Amy Hest	shuffle, swoop
Mud City: A Flamingo Story	Brenda Guiberson	gorging, migrate, scoop
Stars Beneath Your Bed	April Pulley Sayre	crumbling, flakes, spread
Stellaluna	Janell Cannon	confused, embarrassing, obey
Tacky the Penguin	Helen Lester	chanting, odd, companion
The Biggest Nose	Kathy Caple	commotion, swollen
The Great Graph Contest	Loreen Leedy	common, results
The Great Fuzz Frenzy	Janet Stevens and Susan Stevens Crummel	scattered, frenzy, ridiculous
The Pickle Patch Bathtub	Frances Kennedy	gather, durable
The Wolf Who Cried Boy	Bob Hartman	peered, shrugged, mischievous
Wanted: Best Friend	A. M. Monson	hobbled, sailed, klutz
We Live Here Too! Kids Talk About Good Citizenship	Nancy Loewen	debating, pack rat, ignore
What Do You Do When Something Wants to Eat You?	Steve Jenkins	startles, harmless
Wilfrid Gordon McDonald Partridge	Mem Fox	speckled, precious
Wow! It's Great Being a Duck	Joan Rankin	waddled, scrumptious, snout

Opportunity Knocks

Teaching young children doesn't mean that it's impossible to have sophisticated—or pumped up—conversations with them. Interjecting "grown-up" words into your daily banter with students is an easy, spontaneous way to increase their speaking vocabularies—just remember to take advantage of the opportunities.

I Need Help

If one of your students says to you, "I really don't get this. I've *tried* every way I know to find the *answer* to this *problem*," you might reply, "Tommy, it sounds to me like you're feeling *frustrated* because you've *attempted* everything you know how to do and still can't find the *solution* to the *equation*. Let's solve it together." In this situation, you are validating Tommy's feelings, but restating them with more sophisticated vocabulary. Chances like this could come up 20 times a day or more—be ready for them.

Anyone, Anyone?

An opportunity to feed your students' vocabulary might not be as involved as the situation described above. For example, the next time you get a paper with no name on it, hold it up and say, "I've got an *anonymous* paper here. There's no name on it so I don't know whose it is." When having conversations, it is important not only to use new words but also to scaffold them with less complex explanations.

Positive Words

Students love to get compliments from you, so why not use these positive conversations to interject some unfamiliar words? Perhaps Colleen comes to school with a hair ribbon that is full of beads, sequins, and glitter. You could say in passing, "Colleen, that's a snazzy hair ribbon you have on today."

Colleen will no doubt want to know what snazzy means and you'll, of course, explain it to her. Count on Colleen to immediately tell one of her close pals what you said about her hair ribbon and what it means.

There are many other opportunities for you to insert pumped-up vocabulary into the daily grind. Here are a few.

Describe a student who helped two others solve a disagreement as a *mediator*.

Label the settlement of a disagreement *judicious*.

Tell students who are working hard that they are being *industrious*.

Remark on how *flexible* your students are on the playground equipment.

Congratulate them on a quick classroom cleanup by calling them *efficient*.

A student who remembers his library books is *responsible*.

A child who is consoling a classmate is being *empathetic* or *compassionate*.

Label a student *inventive* when she comes up with a new way to solve a math problem.

Ask students to bring a *writing implement* to the rug area.

A fabulous book to share that gives sweet, cookie-centered, kid-friendly definitions of 22 sophisticated words is *Cookies: Bite-Size Life Lessons* by Amy Krouse Rosenthal. It's sure to please.

Where the Words Are

Vocabulary acquisition happens most easily when children are exposed to words in oral situations and are given avenues to revisit and develop their word sense both independently and with peers. Making resources available, such as those listed below, will strengthen vocabulary understanding and encourage the use of colorful words in conversation and later on in written text.

Idioms

Working with idioms can be great fun for your students because many of these expressions are inherently silly. Here are a few excellent, kid-friendly titles to get your idiom instruction under way. Keep books like these in an accessible spot so that any time you have an extra minute, you can share one with your students and discuss what the words actually mean.

In a Pickle and Other Funny Idioms by Marvin Terban

Punching the Clock: Funny Action Idioms by Marvin Terban

Super Silly Sayings That Are Over Your Head: A Children's Illustrated Book of Idioms by Catherine Snodgrass

To give your students even more experience with idioms, make a class book. Using a 12 x 18-inch piece of construction paper, divided in half with a vertical line, each student writes the idiom at the top or bottom of the paper (or you can provide them with the idioms). On the first half of the paper, students draw the literal meaning of the idiom. On the second half, they draw or write what the idiom means. If the idiom is "it's raining cats and dogs," the students would draw cats and dogs coming out of the sky on the left and a pouring rain on the right. If they want to write what the idiom means, help them choose the words to do that.

Introduction to a Thesaurus

Ask your students to give you a word, then look it up in a thesaurus and read some of the alternatives. Make appropriately leveled thesauri available for students to use and help them create their own for words

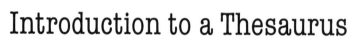

they use too often. Give each student a copy of My Personal Pocket Thesaurus (see pages 66–67) to help them get started.

Personal Writing Dictionaries

Each child can create his own dictionary of words he uses when writing (see Wonderful Words to Use When I Write, pages 64–65). Once the dictionaries are in use, ask children to look in them first for the word they want. If it is not there, they can bring their dictionaries to you or another adult and ask for the word to be added. This creates a usable link between the words you are gradually adding to your students' listening and speaking vocabularies and their writing vocabularies.

Books About Words

Check out these supercreative, sometimes silly titles and your students will love words even more.

BOOK LINKS

Donavan's Word Jar by Monalisa DeGross

Hairy, Scary, Ordinary by Brian Cleary

Miss Alaineus by Debra Frasier

Pig, Pigger, Piggest by Rick Walton

Slide and Slurp, Scratch and Burp by Brian Cleary

Sparkle and Spin by Ann and Paul Rand

The Weighty Word Book by Paul M. Levitt, Douglas A. Burger, and
   Elissa S. Guralnick

Why the Banana Split by Rick Walton

Other Possibilities

◎ Add theme-related ABC books or dictionaries with strong visual support to your classroom library or dictionary shelf. Have conversations with your students about familiar subjects and general categories and dig deeper into their meanings. While *boat* is a word that is familiar to most of your students, they may not know about the variety of boats manufactured (sailboat, rowboat, powerboat, canoe, kayak, and so forth).

◎ Create crossword puzzles that incorporate vocabulary words you want to review and reinforce. Crossword puzzles allow students to review meanings of words in a different way. There are a number of excellent Web sites that offer free downloads, including <u>crosswordpuzzlegames. com</u>, <u>puzzlemaker.discoveryeducation.com,</u> and <u>funbrain.com.</u>

Making the Walls Work

Word walls can be valuable tools for reinforcing oral vocabulary with young children. Many teachers successfully use the traditional format, arranged alphabetically, and include words children use in their writing as well as familiar word families. You can have more than one word wall growing at a time, however, so consider a category word wall.

Category Word Walls

The ability to categorize words is an important skill for learners. Get your students involved in building a category word wall. This concept is similar to a traditional word wall except that instead of being listed alphabetically, words are listed under specific categories. You may wish to start the year with a few categories and words already posted, or you may choose to begin this with your students. Either way, students can add new words as the year goes on. If you don't have wall space available for a word wall or if it becomes too full, you can create category baskets or file folders, placing the words (and maybe illustrations to go with them) inside.

For a more interactive approach, play oral riddle games with your students. For example, you might say, "I'm thinking of a word that is in the category of *clothing*. This is not something you would wear during winter. What is the word?" In this case, it's *sandals*.

People	Nature	Transportation	Clothing	Weather
sister	air	tugboat	shawl	windy
cousin	water	jet	sandals	humid
	soil		beret	
	pollen			

All Around I Hear

The concept of environmental print is not a new one, but in recent years the research has shown how important it is not only to use it but also to expand it. Your young readers will benefit from seeing words everywhere they go, but they will benefit even more if you incorporate enhanced or pumped-up environmental labels into your daily routines and conversations with them.

Environmental print is a natural teacher that is easily expanded at any time. For example, you can label items on posters and charts that are already hanging in your room. In the beginning of the year, you may want to start out with the basics, which will vary according to the grade you teach. For kindergartners, use labels like *window*, *door*, and *sink*; for first through third graders, extend them to include *counter*, *cabinet*, *closet*, and so forth. (The word cards on pages 68–71 will help you get started.)

You can even create bilingual labels for your English language learners. As the year progresses, rename things in your room. Keep the first word card and add a second one (a good way to differentiate), or simply replace the original label with a new one. For example, a door could be renamed *exit*; a desk, *individual work station*; a library area, *reading lounge*; and a computer table, *technology center*. Point out these new labels to students when appropriate, but don't be surprised if they beat you to it and notice the differences right away! More important, use these upgraded labels when you speak. Instead of saying, "Line up at the door," start saying, "Line up at the exit."

You may also want to consider revamping the labels you use on your daily schedule and job chart. Because the labels are so familiar, your students will easily assimilate the new words you use orally by linking them to prior knowledge, and that's one of the best ways to get children to internalize new

phone	wall
glue	rug
scissors	hook
markers	counters
crayons	shelf
pencils	computer
light	stapler
tape	board

eaker	desk
rcom	table
tile	paper
inge	blocks
n	books
	clock
outlet	window
door	chair

vocabulary. So, your mailbox helper might become a *messenger*; your paper passer, a *materials distributor* or *resource officer*; your helper for the day, a *concierge*. On your schedule, a morning meeting label could be replaced with *daily assembly* and science with *research and experiment*. Be sure you frequently verbalize the new names for things so they become a part of your students' listening and speaking vocabularies.

Questions, Anyone?

Asking questions can help your students build their oral vocabularies because it requires them to employ high-level thinking skills like evaluation, application, and analysis. Here are some kid-tested question-and-answer activities to get you going.

Would You Rather?

In this game you ask questions of your students using one or two of your vocabulary words. To make a choice and answer each question, children need to know what the words mean. Once students get the hang of this, they may want to try asking the questions of each other in small groups. If two of your words were *nibble* and *devour*, for example, the question might be: *Would you rather nibble on a candy bar or devour it?* If your two words were *shabby* and *exquisite*, the question might be: *Would you rather have a shabby house or an exquisite one?* You can also use this activity with just one word. If the word is *gnaw* you might ask: *Would you rather gnaw a shoe or a hot dog?*

Question Quad

A quick way to review a word, the Question Quad consists of four question stems that will be connected to that word:

When would you . . . ?

Who would most likely . . . ?

Where would you . . . ?

Why might you . . . ?

If the word is *disturbed*, an example might be:

When would you not want to be disturbed? Possible answers might be when you are sleeping, studying for a test, or talking on the phone.

Who would most likely disturb you?

Where would you expect to be disturbed?

Why might you get disturbed?

Have You Ever?

In this activity children are asked to think of a time when a word—a verb in particular—has applied to them or someone they know. At the very least, they will think of situations when a person would act out the word. Perhaps a new verb might be *sneaked*. Ask your students if they can recall a time when they might have sneaked a cookie from the cookie jar on the counter, sneaked up on a butterfly to try and catch it, or sneaked up on a parent and said, "BOO!" You can also ask them to describe a situation where a person would need to sneak (for example, into a sleeping baby's room to check on her or around the house to look for holiday packages).

Talking Back

In order for deep vocabulary acquisition to occur, children need not only to hear interesting words but also to think about them, apply prior knowledge to their use, and talk about them. (Beck, McKeown, and Kucan, 2002) Talking Back allows students to do all of these. The responses that children offer can vary according to your wishes—just remember, keep it interesting. Here's how it goes.

You have just finished reading Judy Sierra's *Counting Crocodiles* during a math lesson. One word that caught your attention was *scolded*.

◎ First, review the meaning of the word as it relates to the context of the story.

◎ Then tell stuents about a time you were scolded as a child.

◎ After that, ask a few children to tell about a time they were scolded or saw someone else getting scolded.

◎ Finally, offer a variety of scenarios verbally. If the person in the story would likely get scolded, ask the children to say, "You'll get scolded for that" and shake their fingers in the air. If the individual would not get scolded, they can say, "That's okay" and give a thumbs-up sign.

Here's another example. You have read Mem Fox's *Wilfrid Gordon McDonald Partridge* and have chosen the word *errands* from the text to discuss with your students.

◎ First, review the word and how it was used in the story (Mr. Tippett ran errands for Miss Mitchell).

◎ Then describe some errands you might run on a Saturday morning.

◎ After that, ask students to describe some errands they have gone on with their moms or dads (to the bank, the post office, or the supermarket, for example).

◎ Finally, offer other examples. If it's an errand, children can say, "Yup, that's an errand." If it's not an errand (such as going to a movie, taking a bike ride, playing a computer game), they can reply, "No way—that's not an errand."

Show Me The Meaning

In order to really "own" a word, children need to have multiple exposures to it in a variety of contexts. The more modalities you can access when teaching a new word, the more likely children will be able to use it on their own. Getting children's bodies involved is a good way to begin. This works particularly well with action words or words that are associated with emotions. Here are some examples.

While reading *Franklin's Bad Day* by Paulette Bourgeois, you come across the word *miserable*. After the story is completed, remind your students that Franklin was feeling miserable in the beginning of the story because he was missing his friend Otter. Show them the front cover, which portrays a very unhappy turtle, and repeat the word *miserable*. Then ask students to tell you about a time when they felt miserable (for example, when they were sick, when a friend moved away, or when someone teased them). Next have students actually show you with their faces and their bodies what they would look like if they were feeling miserable.

You are reading *The Emperor's Egg* by Martin Jenkins to your students because it is part of your reading program. The author mentions the word *waddle*. Once you have finished the story, see if students know what the word means. Ask them to recall what waddled in the story and why (the daddy penguin with the egg on his feet and the penguins when they traveled). Encourage a discussion about other living things that waddle or something else they have seen waddle. Finally, ask students to waddle to a particular destination in your classroom.

BOOK LINKS

Use the following books and words for more Show Me the Meaning:

Brave Irene by William Steig: *shuffling*

Chrysanthemum by Kevin Henkes: *longingly*

Stellaluna by Janell Cannon: *clutched*

The Great Fuzz Frenzy by Janet Stevens and Susan Crummel: *plucked*

The Little Scarecrow Boy by Margaret Wise Brown: *fierce*

The Wolf Who Cried Boy by Bob Hartman: *peered*

Talking While We Work

If you've gotten rid of your dramatic play space, *bring it back!* A dramatic play area is the perfect spot for children to use grown-up tools and have grown-up conversations. It provides an excellent opportunity for valuable oral vocabulary practice.

When you introduce the objects and tools they'll use, and when students interact with someone whose oral language abilities are more advanced than their own, such as a parent volunteer, a teacher, or another student, they'll be hearing new words and repeating them in context. For example, as you introduce items being placed in your make-believe restaurant, you might show students forks and knives, but call them *eating utensils*; napkins and tablecloths become *table linens*; and dinner becomes an *entrée* on the menu.

Be sure to make time in your day for dramatic play. You can incorporate it into your center schedule, offer it on a daily rotation basis, or use it as an option during choice time.

Situation or Location	Objects or Tools
Restaurant	menus, notepads for orders, to-go bags, Styrofoam containers, specials board, pens, telephone, reservation book, table settings
Post Office	envelopes, stamps, rubber stamps, ZIP code listing, phone book, cubbies for sorting mail, junk mail, adding machine, blue button-up shirts
Hardware Store	carpenters' aprons, paper bags, buckets, plastic pipes, cash register, empty paint cans, appropriate tools, shovel, lawn bags, flowerpots, rope, keys, price signs, paint-chip color samples
Business Office	phones, computer keyboard, pads, pens, file folders and cabinet, desks and chairs, product brochures, stapler, tape, calculator

Conversation Station

Allowing children to talk with each other is valuable. Every child brings a background of some kind, perhaps even a relative expertise, to the classroom (one student may know more about outer space than most adults!), and the best way for them to share their knowledge is most often with their voices. Be sure, however, to model what their voices should sound like and provide some examples of times when it would be okay to talk while working. Listen to their conversations and make note of any good vocabulary candidates you can focus on at another time.

Here are some natural but structured opportunities for students to talk with each other.

Snapshot

It's never too early to begin your vocabulary instruction. In the beginning of the year, ask children to bring pictures that depict their families or another special part of their lives to school. Break students into small groups and allow time for each child to share her photo and for each member of the group to ask a question about it.

I Love Books!

A favorite or familiar book is a great conversation starter. Most every child has a deep love for one particular book, so let him share it with a buddy. His passion for the book may be contagious and encourage other students to check it out. Remember, even nonreaders can talk about a book by sharing the pictures and their observations.

Go Van Gogh

Original artwork is full of personal touches and thus makes a good vehicle for conversation. Provide a variety of mediums and materials to your students (pom-poms, pipe cleaners, buttons, Cray-Pas, and whatever else is handy) and give them adequate time to create a piece of artwork. Once completed, pair students for a five-minute art exhibition where they can explain their creation to a friend.

Morning News

Make this a Monday morning ritual. Assign a few students for each Monday morning of the month to be news anchors, making sure everyone has an opportunity to share by month's end. When you gather together to start the day, ask that week's news anchors to talk about something they saw or did over the past weekend.

I Hear an Idea

Sometimes a storybook you like or one you have to use does not offer a plethora of oral vocabulary "moments." In this situation, look for a concept, event, or idea in the story that can be explained through the use of a new vocabulary word.

For example, David Shannon's *Good Boy, Fergus!* contains very simple and very few words between its covers. The illustrations are terrific and the main character, a West Highland Terrier, is adorable—both good hooks for kids. Upon first glance, this fun book offers no candidates for listening and speaking vocabulary instruction. After considering the main idea of the book (Fergus being a less-than-perfect dog), you realize that the words *obedient* and *disobedient* are a perfect fit with the book. Both words are useful in a variety of contexts so they are easily revisited, and *disobedient* also allows for some conversation about prefixes (in this case *dis-*).

Here are some other books that lend themselves to teaching a vocabulary word based on concept and not necessarily actual word content.

BOOK LINKS

Actual Size by Steve Jenkins: *extremely*

Barfburger Baby, I Was Here First by Paula Danziger: *envious*

Emile by Kurt Futterer: *abstract* (art)

Hunwick's Egg by Mem Fox: *companion*

I Am America by Charles R. Smith, Jr.: *preference*

I Saw an Ant on the Railroad Track by Joshua Prince: *compassion*

Me on the Map by Joan Sweeney: *location*

Tacky the Penguin by Helen Lester: *individuality*

The Hello, Goodbye Window by Norton Juster: *generation*

The Skin You Live In by Michael Tyler: *diversity*

The OK Book by Amy Krouse Rosenthal: *adequate*

Wanted: Best Friend by A. M. Monson: *compatible*

What Do You Do When Something Wants to Eat You? by Steve Jenkins: *instinct*

What's So Terrible About Swallowing an Apple Seed? By Harriet Lerner and Susan Goldhor: *dilemma*

You Ought to See Herbert's House by Doris Herold Lund: *exaggerate*

Read It to Me Again, Sam

Research tells us that rereading a book whose vocabulary has been taught explicitly through direct instruction tremendously increases the likelihood that the words will remain with the child over extended periods of time. The rereading does not need to take place all in one week; it could be done as many as six times over the course of a few months or even the entire school year.

Rereading not only promotes greater oral vocabulary development but also improves fluency, listening comprehension, and possibly knowledge of a topic, so you get a bigger bang for your instructional buck. Each time you reread a text, your students' understanding is taken to a new level because they are able to pay closer attention to smaller details, and you can encourage discussions beyond the general scope of the text.

Here are six steps for rereading for vocabulary retention.

1. The first time you read a book, complete the sequence of steps described in Talking Back on page 25 for words you want to teach.

2. The next time you read it, review the vocabulary you taught the first time, write those words on the board, and ask students to focus on finding details or events (either in illustrations or in the words themselves) that relate to one of the words you taught originally. Allow for open discussion during the reading.

3. During the third reading, remind students of the words and have them use facial and silent body movements to represent events that relate to the words or the words themselves when heard (see Show Me the Meaning, page 26).

4. After reading the book a fourth time, ask for volunteers to retell a part of the story that relates to one of the vocabulary words. Other students can add details to the partial retelling if you wish.

5. Following the fifth reading, have students choose one of the words you taught and draw the part of the story that best depicts that word. Allow students to share their artwork and explain how their drawings depict the words they chose. Mount the drawings and words on a bulletin board so they remain in front of your students.

6. The sixth rereading can simply be reading for pleasure. Be sure to review the words you started with all those readings ago and allow students to share anything they noticed from the story that they hadn't noticed before.

Here are a few ideas to keep your rereading efforts fresh.

◎ Ask your principal to read the book to your class. New faces and voices add interest, and different readers bring their own inflections and experiences to the reading.

◎ Get a copy of the book on audiocassette and play it for your students. Sometimes you can even find titles that are read by the authors themselves. If you don't want to buy a prerecorded tape, ask a colleague to help you make one and invite your students to guess who the mystery reader is.

◎ Have an older child (maybe one of your former students) read the book to your class. If necessary, give the guest reader the book ahead of time so she can become familiar with the text.

◎ Send out a call for parent-volunteer readers. Even a parent too busy to come on a regular basis can most likely find time for one appearance.

◎ Videotape a reading of the book by another staff member, maybe a teacher students know from a grade younger than yours.

Remember that children who come from low-literacy backgrounds will benefit most from the use of repeated read-alouds in the classroom because their exposure to more elaborate and unusual vocabulary outside of school may be limited or nonexistent.

PUMP UP THE VOLUME

Mapping the Meaning

The English language is full of words that have multiple meanings or uses. According to the *American Heritage Dictionary*, the word *call*, for example, has more than 50! So it's important to talk about those words with your students. Use word maps to untangle these words and their meanings when the need arises. Be sure to give an example of each meaning as it is added to the map by using it in a sentence or context familiar to your students. Display the maps after they have been completed so that students can refer to them when necessary, or make a smaller version of each map available in a three-ring binder in your classroom library. When possible, add pictures to the maps to reinforce meanings. In the map below, pictures of a toy top, a spider's web, and a spinning wheel could be added to further clarify each use of the word. *Kidspiration* is a great technology tie-in to this type of vocabulary development. Use the reproducible on page 72 to start mapping.

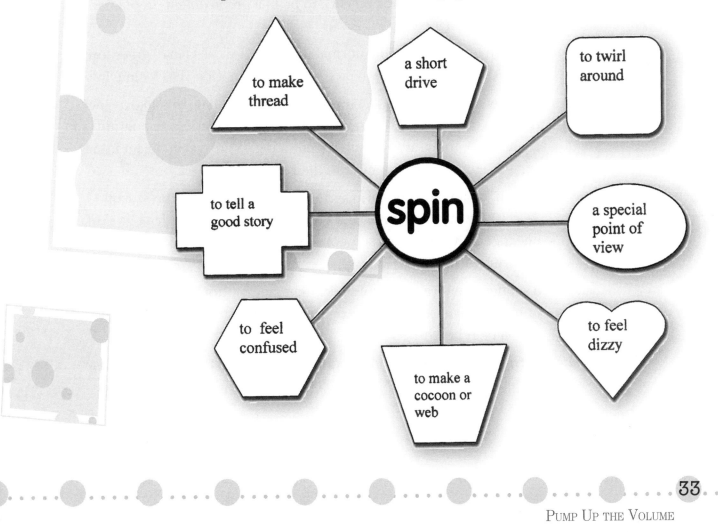

Here are a few more words with multiple meanings to consider using with the map.

bill: a bird's beak, paper money, charges for goods or services, a proposed law, to meet requirements (fill the bill), to book a performer

bow: a tool for shooting arrows, an instrument for playing the violin, a ribbon worn in the hair, a curve in something, a decoration on a present

cold: a temperature lower than expected, not warmed up, unfriendly, lacking feelings, a viral infection, an unlucky streak in sports, stopped completely or unexpectedly

crack: to break without falling apart, a strange change in a person's voice, an attempt (take a crack at it), to solve (crack the case), to break into (crack the code, crack a safe)

drum: an instrument, to tap continually, to play a rhythm, to get business (drum up), part of the inner ear, to instill by repetition (drum it into them)

fall: to drop down, the season after summer, to become lower (fall in price), to take place on (her birthday falls on a Sunday this year), to be tricked or to like or become interested in (fall for)

fix: to fasten firmly, to be set on in your mind, to look intently at something, to repair, to prepare (fix a meal), to be in a predicament, to put back in order or arrangement

low: not high or tall, below the normal level, shallow, less in degree (low speed), deep in pitch (low voice), negative emotion (I'm feeling low)

run: to go by moving the legs faster than walking, to flee, to make a quick trip (run to the store), to compete in a race or election, to operate (run a machine), to unravel (a run in a stocking), to drive an object into something else (run the car into the garbage can)

spring: to leap, to appear suddenly (spring up), a coil of wire, the season following winter, a source of water from the ground, to leak unexpectedly, to pay for someone else or something, to bounce slightly (a spring in your step)

stroke: a sudden event (a stroke of luck), repeated motions in swimming or rowing, a mark made by a pen, to pet an animal, a movement made with a paintbrush

turn: to rotate, to move around or partly around (turn the key), to change direction or position, to change to another form (the rain turned to snow), to wrench (turn your ankle)

Timing Is Everything

When using read-alouds to teach new listening and speaking vocabulary, hold off on introducing the words you plan to teach until you come across them in the text. That way comprehension isn't compromised by a child's attempt to recall a definition you provided seven pages ago. Operating this way also allows you to build an immediate, universal, and useful context for your students because you can relate it right to the story. It's okay while reading aloud to stop briefly and discuss the word, its connotation, and its meaning within the story. Introducing words ahead of time should be saved for situations when students will be reading on their own and not have you available to scaffold for them.

Some words are important for general comprehension but may not necessarily be candidates for your oral vocabulary instruction. When you're confronted with one of those words, stop reading and provide as brief a definition as possible before continuing on. Further discussion is not merited here. This supports your students' comprehension efforts without giving them more information than they really need.

For example, while reading Patricia MacLachlan's *All the Places to Love*, you will come to a phrase that reads ". . . where marsh hawks skimmed over the land . . . ." You might simply say, "Skimmed means they flew just barely above it" and continue with the reading.

Nonfiction books are full of these kinds of words, but be careful not to stop too many times to explain words. Stick to those that are truly essential for your students' understanding of the concept. If you are reading a book on weather and it says a blizzard can cause deep, drifting snow, there is no need to define *drifting*. The word that comes before it, *deep*, provides a helpful context clue. Even if students do not pick up on the clue, knowing what *drifting* means is not necessary for them to understand that a blizzard creates a lot of snow. However, if you are sharing a book about reptiles that states that snakes use the muscles attached to their spines to move, your students really do need to know what a spine is to better understand a snake's movement.

Predict & Prove

Most children will have something to share if you ask, "What do you think is going to happen in this book?" Use that interest along with some choice vocabulary words and phrases and an air of mystery to elicit predictions from your students about a book's setting, characters, problem, events, and ending.

Choose a book that you know your students are not familiar with. And don't show the book's cover when you do this activity—that may provide too many clues. Here's the procedure.

Write a book's title on chart paper along with some words and phrases you have selected from it. Read them to or with your students and explain any words necessary. For example, the illustration below shows what you might do with *Little Honey Bear and the Smiley Moon*, a book by Gillian Lobel.

Little Honey Bear and the Smiley Moon

glittering
hare
squeaked
flurries
slipped
quivered
tucked
hooray

Also write on chart paper the story elements you want your students to address:

Characters

Setting

Problem

Events

Ending

Based on the title and the words provided, ask students to make oral predictions about the different story elements and which words made them think a specific event would happen. Some predictions for the example on the preceding page might include:

The hare quivered because he's afraid of the dark.

Little Honey Bear was tucked in bed and could see the moon glittering from his bedroom.

Little Honey Bear sniffed after he slipped on something.

Record as many ideas as you have time for, making sure that there is at least one prediction for each element. Then read the story to your students and check their predictions either as you go or when the story is complete.

A Picture's Worth 1,000 Spoken Words

Okay, maybe not 1,000, but photographs are a great way to boost your students' exposure to word-rich environments and ownership of listening and speaking vocabulary. Children will absorb vocabulary more readily if they have multiple and personal connections to its origin or use. Taking pictures of field-trip sights or people and places within your community is a valuable vocabulary builder because you can have lively discussions with your students about what they saw and experienced.

But that's not all. After you've taken the pictures and printed them, you need to label the key aspects of each snapshot. The labels to be added should be generated through discussion with your students as soon as possible. Once they are labeled, place the photos in a similarly themed dramatic play area. For instance, if you recently visited the post office, you can set up your drama center to reflect that part of the community. Given the opportunity, children will begin to use words specific to that location in their oral exchanges while they are engaged in creative play. If visiting a particular location is not an option, use photos from nonfiction books and other informational text instead, such as brochures, menus, maps, magazines, etc.

Here is a list of possible places for photo opportunities and likely labels to get you started.

Post Office: *postage scale, postmark, postmaster, priority*

Farm: *tractor, crops, irrigation, barn*

Supermarket: *clerk, receipt, scanner, produce, dairy products, register*

Movie Theater: *balcony, aisle, ticket stub, concession stand, turnstile*

Restaurant: *hostess, entrée, beverage, appetizer, server, check, gratuity*

Museum: *curator, collection, specimen, artifact, conservation room*

Amusement Park: *attractions, admission pass, cotton candy*

Photo Finish

Some vocabulary words that you choose may lend themselves to an action or an expression. Adding visual support to oral vocabulary words will help students understand their meanings more easily when they hear them and use those words more confidently when they speak. With a digital camera, take and print pictures of your students acting out different vocabulary words and post them on a bulletin board. For example, if one of the words you are focusing on is *surrounded*, then you could take a picture of one student completely surrounded by other children, books, or blocks. Ask your students for input about what the picture should look like. This type of discussion will reinforce their understanding of the word. Add a label to the picture, such as "Jack is *surrounded* by his classmates." Be sure your label identifies or highlights the focus word in some way; write it in italics, in a different color, in uppercase letters, or in some other way that makes it noticeable.

Vocabulary Gallery

Attaching pictures or symbols to vocabulary words is a great way to differentiate for your students and give everyone's brain another way to recall the meanings of words, thus fostering more frequent use in oral contexts. After spending time learning a new word, ask students to draw what that word looks like to them. For example, if you asked students to illustrate the word *sniff*, you might get pictures of a cat sniffing a mouse hole, a child sniffing flowers, a woman sniffing a bottle of perfume, a dog sniffing the ground, and a group of adults sniffing hot dogs at a barbecue. Invite children to verbally share their artwork in small groups and encourage conversations about each other's work.

Post the word with the illustrations until you are ready to put another word on the board. Then bind the illustrations together, title the book *Sniff*, and place it in your classroom library. By making your student-created book available, you'll provide other opportunities for students to talk about that word at a later time when they are looking at the pictures with a peer. If you have focused on two or three words from a particular storybook, let the children choose which word they want to illustrate or assign each child one of the words.

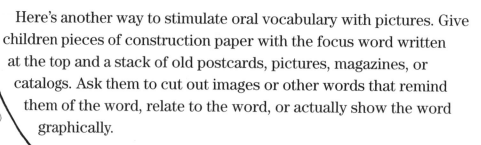

Here's another way to stimulate oral vocabulary with pictures. Give children pieces of construction paper with the focus word written at the top and a stack of old postcards, pictures, magazines, or catalogs. Ask them to cut out images or other words that remind them of the word, relate to the word, or actually show the word graphically.

Allow time for students to share their interpretations with the group. Their reasons for why they have included certain graphics will require them to do some higher-level thinking and speaking to show you how well they understand the word. In addition, the conversations the group will have about the word will help others remember it more easily. Invite students to confer with you at any time about their choices—you are the most literate person in the room.

Dig Deep with Concept Dictionaries

A concept dictionary contains words related to a specific topic, for example, *ocean life*. Creating concept dictionaries is easy and interactive, and they play an important role in deepening your students' understanding of a familiar, general word or category. This deeper comprehension enables them to understand conversations more clearly and to be more precise when they speak. Students can make individual dictionaries or you can make one together for the entire class to use. Either way, concept dictionaries will become valuable resources for your students during thematic units of study throughout the year.

Use any size paper or the reproducible provided on page 73. To create a dictionary, you will need pictorial representations of the words you plan to include. These can be pictures clipped from magazines or other sources or illustrations by your students. The word-and-picture pages should then be assembled in alphabetical order. If your students are already reading, you may wish to add a brief definition to all or some of the pages, but do this only if the object can be explained in words they are already familiar with.

Place the completed concept dictionary near other books and resources that are relevant to the unit you are currently studying. This illustration shows what a double-page spread in a concept dictionary might look like for a unit on ocean life.

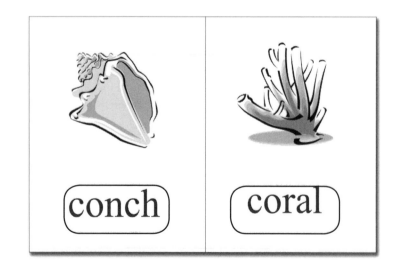

Category Club

Enroll your students in the Category Club and take them on a "trip" from the general to the specific. It's an easy, interactive way to stretch oral vocabularies and add detail to your students' conversations now and to their writing later on.

Begin with a general word like *home*, write it on a piece of poster board, and hang the poster board so it can be seen by everyone. Discuss different kinds of homes, including those in other countries and cultures and different types of animal homes like dens, burrows, nests, and doghouses. Then ask students to find examples of all kinds of homes in magazines, newspapers, or catalogs. Have them cut out and bring you their pictures as they find each one. Tell them they can also bring in a photograph of their own homes if they wish. (Mary Ann Hoberman's book *A House Is a House for Me* is an excellent tie-in for this.)

Encourage conversations among students while they are involved in this activity. They are likely to make personal connections to some of these homes and will want to share these connections with their peers. Remember, their strength lies in their oral abilities right now. Conversing and relating personal stories will reinforce the meanings of new words. While they are looking, cutting out, and delivering pictures, paste some select pictures of homes onto the poster board. When your poster board is nearly full, ask students to join you. Talk about the different features of each home and label each kind with your students' help.

You can even choose a general animal label like *dog* or *cat* and have your students find pictures of these animals in advertisements, old calendars, or on the Internet. Labeling different breeds of cats and dogs will increase vocabularies and interest in learning more about these animals. You'll also hear lots of conversations based on personal connections as children discuss their grandmother's Persian cat or their neighbor's Dalmatian! Other words you might consider using are *snack, cookie, toy, car, shoe, flower, boat,* and *book*.

Sense-ational Strategies

Getting students to be aware of and use interesting words when they speak will also encourage children to listen for them and use them in their own writing—any teacher's dream! Involving children's senses in this quest increases their opportunities for success because they are already familiar with the five senses, and familiarity helps the brain attach meaning to new words.

Five-Senses Snacking

Bring bags of potato chips, gummy worms, graham crackers, and various fresh fruits or vegetables to school. (Be sure to check first with your school nurse for any allergy concerns.) Give each child a few of each kind of food. Have students brainstorm words that reflect how each food feels, looks, smells, tastes, and even sounds when eaten, and record their words on a five-senses chart or word map. This will foster lively conversations and whet your students' appetites for stimulating word choices—literally!

Pumpkin Exploration

This activity is most easily done in the fall, but if you can't do it when pumpkins are available, try using a large honeydew melon at any time of the year. Cut out an opening in the top (stem end) of a fresh pumpkin and replace the top. Make two large paper pumpkins with orange construction paper and staple them together on the left side so they open like a book. Post the paper-pumpkin "book" on your chalkboard and put the real pumpkin on a stool or desk in front of it. Allow each child to look closely at the outside only and touch it if they wish. Ask each one to say a few words to describe how it looks and feels on the outside. Record their words on the outside of the pumpkin book. After everyone

has had a turn, take the top off the fresh pumpkin and let each student in turn stick her hand inside. Ask her to say a few words that describe how this part of the pumpkin feels, looks, or smells. Open the pumpkin book and record these words on the inside. With your scaffolding, the words they use will stretch into rich vocabulary opportunities.

Round Robin Senses

Get your students outside (or at least out of the classroom) to use their five senses. Have them sit in a circle and ask each one to tell you something they hear, see, smell, or feel. Record their answers on the Round Robin Senses reproducible (see page 74) and brainstorm with them to come up with more descriptive vocabulary. For example, if Alli mentions that she hears voices across the street, you might ask her if they sound excited, grouchy, delighted, or booming. Also ask if the sound is something familiar to her or if it's a different or new sound. Then record her response under the appropriate heading. You may not be able to fill in the *taste* box every time, but a child might say she tastes her flavored lip balm or something to that effect.

Round Robin Senses

	Familiar	Different
Sight		large bird
Smell		sour
Taste	blueberries	
Hearing		chirping
Touch	damp grass	

Sing It, Say It

Children are naturally attracted to the rhyme and rhythm of music and poetry—both powerful tools for fostering vocabulary growth. Using these also addresses the right side of the brain (most vocabulary instruction utilizes the left side) so you are helping more students to access and retain information based on their learning styles. Songs and poems are excellent choices for instructing students who are English language learners for the same reasons. Dr. Lucy Guglielmino provides these basic criteria for using rhythmic pieces in our primary vocabulary instruction:

◎ The piece should be easy to read or sing.

◎ The content should be related to the current unit of study.

◎ Students should be able to see the words any time you use the piece.

◎ The piece should contain repeating words, word families, choruses, or verses.

◎ Always follow up with activities and discussions about words whenever you use the piece.

Consider the possibilities for listening and speaking vocabulary (some have been underlined) in the following poem.

Elephant Skin

by Laureen Reynolds

Do you <u>suppose</u> an elephant
Is happy with his skin?
The <u>crinkles</u> and the <u>wrinkles</u>
That are <u>sprinkled</u> thick and thin?
Do you suppose an elephant,
Providing he had <u>loot</u>,
Would find a haberdashery
And buy a brand-new suit?

You and your students can set this poem to rap music (anything that rhymes can be rapped!), show what crinkled, wrinkled skin might look like (have kids tightly crumple a paper bag and then open it up), or discuss what else might have a texture or appearance similar to elephant skin.

If Words Could Talk

We want words to take on lives of their own for our students, so why not bring them to life in the classroom? The more easily students adopt new words, the more quickly they will use them in their listening and speaking vocabularies.

Since students absorb vocabulary words more readily when they are reinforced through pictures, try this artful way of bringing words to life. Using a select list of words you have focused on in the past, ask each student to draw a different word in a way that explains its definition. The examples below show possible outcomes for this activity. Once completed, post these living, breathing words on your bulletin board for everyone to enjoy—and use!

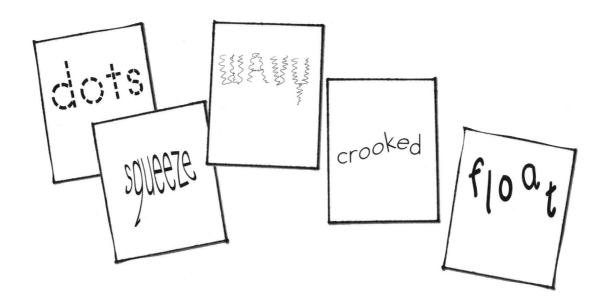

Let the Games Begin

The research tells us that playing games encourages brain growth and thus increases learning. Games that involve substantial physical movement assist the brain in retaining information more readily. When we play games with our students, we also provide differentiation because we are addressing more than one learning style. Games also offer a natural vehicle for focused conversation, so any words you include in a game format will automatically be discussed as students make their way through the play. Conversations may be initiated when two players are trying to figure out if a match is correct, when a player is explaining what she drew, when a small group is guessing a word based on clues, or when you feel the need to make some clarifications for your students.

Whole Group Charades

Using body movements and postures to convey vocabulary words is an excellent way to reach your kinesthetic learners. Children are applying their knowledge of words no matter which end of the game they are on. If you have

spent time building a target-word bulletin board, concept dictionaries, category word walls, or any of the other ideas discussed in this book, these are great sources for words for children to act out. You can also provide words on index cards with picture clues or just whisper clues into a student's ear. If your students are older, divide them into small groups to play. You should join in too. As the most literate person in the room, your interaction with the children and the words has a huge impact on learning. Plus, they will love trying to guess the word you are portraying.

Picture It

This simplified version of the popular game *Pictionary* can be played in large or small groups. Instead of acting out words, this time children are trying to draw clues about them. In the beginning, play as a whole group. Gather children on the rug and assign a student to be the artist. Supply her with large chart paper or your white board and markers, a word, and a corresponding illustration. You may want to have a quick conference with the artist to help her get started and to facilitate the game in any way to achieve success. There is no time limit unless you have older or more able students who want that challenge. You may choose to tell students what category a word falls into to deepen their understanding of that word.

Hot Potato

Children sit in a circle for this game, with one student holding a potato or a tennis ball. Select a category such as occupations and then say a word. If it relates to the category (receptionist, crane operator, dentist), the child holding the potato passes it to someone else. If the word does not relate to the category (monitor, jagged), the child keeps the potato. If necessary, offer help at any point and allow students to coach each other. You might also ask older or more able students to supply words that fit the category.

Pass the Monkey

Another version of a category game, this one is a little more challenging. Children sit or stand in a circle. Holding a toy monkey, you state a category and then ask for a volunteer. That child goes to the middle of the circle and attempts to name five things that fit into the category you named before the monkey gets passed all the way around the circle and back to you. The next volunteer has a more difficult challenge because she is not allowed to repeat anything the first child said. It's your job to keep track of the words that have been used and signal her if something she names is a repeat.

Hot and Cold

For this activity you will need to mentally prepare some sentences ahead of time that go along with one of your vocabulary words. Some of the sentences should use the word correctly and some should not. Each time you say a sentence, the children will say, "That's hot" if you have used the word correctly or "That's cold" if you have not. Make this more fun by having your students fan themselves if it's a hot sentence and hug themselves, shiver, and say "brrrrr" if it's a cold sentence. You can also have them hold up symbols for hot and cold sentences like a picture of a fire or of an ice cube. If your word is *meadow*, a "hot" sentence might be: "The bird flew over the meadow and landed in a nearby tree." A "cold" sentence might be: "We packed up the meadow in the car and brought it home with us."

Category Clap

Children sit or stand in a circle. Provide a category, such as a content area theme like "things related to the desert," and start a beat (by clapping your hands) that your students will do with you. The first student names something that fits in the category, then the next student does, until everyone has had a chance. Children may pass if they wish, but always return to them at the end of a round and give them another chance to respond. The goal is to get all the way around the circle without any repeats.

Keep Your Ears Open

An awareness of words is essential to vocabulary acquisition. Helping our students to develop this takes time, but once they know and love words, they'll be hooked forever.

Encourage your students to "keep their ears open" for words that spark their curiosity during the course of each week. Tell them to listen to people in their lives talking, conversations on television programs or in movies, or stories that an older sibling, parent, or caregiver might read to them. Students who are already reading a bit can also refer to children's magazines like *Highlights* and *High Five,* books at their reading levels, comics, or educational newspapers like *Scholastic News.*

To extend this idea, give your students copies of the Keep Your Ears Open reproducible (see page 75) to use for noting these words and indicating how they happened to encounter them. Spelling doesn't matter at this point, so be sure to tell students not to worry about it. The purpose of the activity is to make them more aware of intriguing, engaging, and fascinating words in their everyday lives. Here's an example of what this might look like.

Name _____   **Week of** _____

Words I heard . . .	on TV	on the computer	in a video game	in a book somebody read to me	my parents say	in a movie	in a store or restaurant
demolish	X		X				
stride				X			
extinct						X	
pungent							X
review		X			X		

Hold the Phone

Homophones are a daily reminder of how tricky the English language can be. Explaining them to young children will increase their listening, reading, speaking, and writing vocabularies.

Due Ewe See What Eye Sea?

Give students homophone practice and create a resource that will be used all year by making homophone cards. Write each word from a homophone pair on a separate index card, making as many different pairs as you want or making one of the same pair for each student. Discuss the differences between the words and provide examples of contexts, enlisting your students' prior knowledge as you do so. Ask students to glue each card of the pair onto a half sheet of white paper. Then have them draw a picture that shows the meaning of each word in the pair and write a sentence using the word if they can. If each child illustrates a different pair of homophones, bind the papers together in alphabetical order and place the book in your library or writing center. If each student makes her own set of the same pair, have her glue the cards into a blank book and store it in her desk or writing folder for future reference.

Here's a list of homophones you may want to try.

arc/ark	nose/knows
bare/bear	pail/pale
bored/board	pain/pane
doe/dough	pair/pear
eight/ate	plain/plane
feet/feat	sea/see
flower/flour	sent/scent
hair/hare	some/sum
here/hear	there/their
hi/high	which/witch
meet/meat	whirled/world
mist/missed	write/right

Use Content Areas, Too

Science, social studies, math, and other content areas can be rich sources of vocabulary. Just be sure that the vocabulary you choose from a specific unit or theme is flexible enough to be used during listening and speaking exchanges and is likely to be encountered in other areas of your students' lives as well.

If Walls Could Talk

Plan for interactive learning in content areas by creating sections of bulletin board for science, social studies, and other major subjects. In each section, staple pictures or posters that are connected to the current unit, theme, or concept your students are learning about and then label some of the posters or pictures. Ask your students to tell you about anything they see in a picture and about things that they think of when they look at it. Then add those labels, extending the conversation as necessary. As your students learn more about the topic, they can add additional labels using sticky notes. If a child names something that isn't pictured but relates to the topic, put those labels around its borders or at the bottom.

Topic Table

Fill a table with lots of reading materials related to a specific theme being studied, like the ocean, to increase oral vocabulary. This strategy stimulates conversations about topics that appeal to your students. Even your nonreaders or those who struggle to read will happily sit down with an engrossing book and a friend and talk about what they see. The table may include magazine or newspaper clippings, easy nonfiction readers, picture books, pictures with captions, and any other printed material about the topic. Check with your school librarian for suggestions. You might want to include real objects as well. So if the theme is oceans, there could be shells, sand dollars, and sea glass on the table. Providing a wide variety of materials also enables you to differentiate your instruction since children can get their hands on materials that are just right for their reading or interest levels. During any free time, encourage children to use the materials on the table and discuss them with a buddy.

Book 'Em

I've spent a lot of time talking about how to use storybooks to enhance vocabulary, so don't forget to employ the same techniques when you read a content-based book to your students (see, for example, Bring in the Books on page 13, Show Me the Meaning on page 26, I Hear an Idea on page 30). There are many excellent titles relating to content-area topics that read like (or actually are) stories, so use them, too! Here are a few.

BOOK LINKS

A Busy Year by Leo Lionni: *seasons, calendar*

Author: A True Story by Helen Lester: *writing process*

Dear Mr. Blueberry by Simon James: *habitats*

Elevator Magic by Stuart Murphy: *subtraction*

If You Decide to Go to the Moon by Faith McNulty: *space*

Mud City: A Flamingo Story by Brenda Guiberson: *life cycles*

Content Area Word Walls

Use a specialized, temporary word wall to increase content area listening and speaking vocabulary. The discussion that revolves around each word when it is placed (or not placed) in a particular category is the most important part of this word wall, so be sure to allow time for that. Just be careful not to get too specialized because you want to keep the vocabulary flexible and accessible to your students. Here are two examples.

WHALES

NAMES	BODY PARTS	FOOD/PREY	DAILY LIFE
right	fin	seals	pods
blue	flipper	walrus	migration
humpback	eye	fish	singing
orca			
gray			

MATH

SHAPES	OPERATIONS	TOOLS	MONEY	UNITS OF MEASURE
oval	addition	ruler	penny	inch
rectangle	subtraction	calculator	nickel	centimeter
cube	multiplication	yardstick	dime	foot
triangle	division		quarter	yard

Brainstorm It

Effective brainstorming starts with you and your students working together. Brainstorm words about a topic that you want your students to write about later, and draw or write these words on the board. Explain some of the additions to the list as you go and add some of your own ideas.

- ◎ Leave the words and pictures on the board for students to refer to when they write. Type or write the brainstormed list and give each student a copy to use if their writing will extend beyond one day.

- ◎ Remind them to add any words they like to their personal dictionaries and give them time to do this.

- ◎ File one copy of each typed list in a three-ring binder. Keep this "brainstorm book" in your classroom library or store the lists alphabetically by topic in a system that's accessible to your students when they want to use a word another time.

- ◎ Use pictures or posters to get your students' brainstorming juices flowing. Post the picture on the board and add sticky notes with words generated by your students. Put the notes in the appropriate places on or around the picture to facilitate use by struggling learners. Leave blank sticky notes out and encourage students to add words to the picture as they think of them during their own writing.

Brainstorming can be purposefully limited as well. Sometimes you may want students to give you only words that are synonyms for a particular word such as *happy* or *small*. Brainstorming can reflect a broader spectrum of word association also, as in the sample on the facing page.

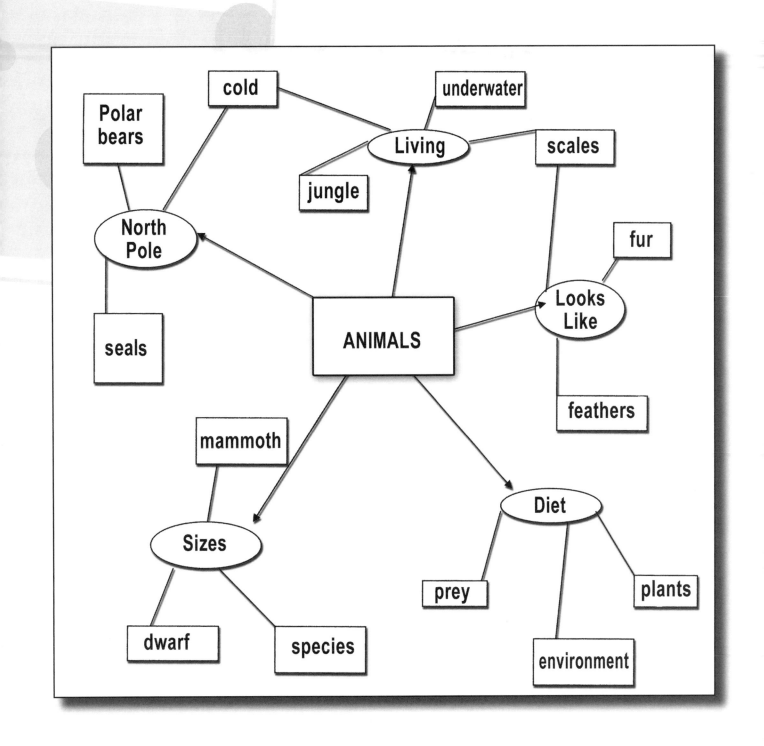

Talk It Out

The ability to sort, label, and categorize words is important to vocabulary acquisition, expansion, and ownership because it requires children to talk with you or within small groups about a word and analyze its characteristics, attributes, and components. Use the Talk It Out reproducible (see page 76) to get your students sorting within general categories.

The illustration below uses transportation as an example, so your instructions might be as follows: Place an X in each box that goes with each mode of transportation. Add some of your own ways to get from one place to another by writing a word or drawing a picture.

Talk It Out

Name __Candice__   Category __Transportation__

Transportation	On land	In the water	In the air	Has wheels	People powered	Fuel powered
car	X			X		X
boat		X			X	X
baby stroller	X			X	X	
hot air balloon			X			X
bicycle	X			X	X	
plane			X	X		X

Meet My Associates

It's important for students to have contexts that are not text-related for new words, so do a little word association with them. Let's say you chose the words *horizon*, *speckled*, and *complimented* from a storybook. Review the meaning of each word with your students and ask them to repeat the words out loud. Then ask, "Which new word goes with the word *sun*?" They should call out "horizon!" You might continue with an explanation of the association: "Yes, *horizon* is right because the sun rises and sets on the horizon."

Your next question might be: "Which new word goes with the word *beautiful*?" One student might say *complimented* because her mother gets complimented on how nice she looks in her dress with the red flowers on it. Another student may decide that *speckled* goes with the word *beautiful* because he found a bird's egg that had speckles on it and he thought it was really pretty. Both of these responses are logical and should be allowed. When students can justify their answers—even if they're different from what you expected— you know that they're thinking about words.

Repeat this strategy as many times as you like, but try to give more than one association for each word so students keep thinking about all of the words.

Center Stage Words

Getting students to become active listening and speaking vocabulary participants can be easier than you may think and it's critical to their development as word aficionados. Keeping new words in plain sight and discussing them frequently will help everyone, including you, to remember what they were, what they mean, and where they were first found.

Create a Center Stage Words bulletin board. Select a spot in your room that can hold up to ten index cards and ten small illustrations. It can be on a door or hanging from a wire—whatever works for your space. Enlist your students' help to build it. Tell them to be on the lookout for exciting words when they are reading to themselves or you are reading to them. A word they thought of when looking at a picture in a book might be a candidate too. Once identified, ask the student who found it to also illustrate the word and write it on an index card, with your help if necessary. You might ring a bell to announce that you are placing a new word on the board, then read it and explain it very briefly. Later students can look at the accompanying illustration to remember what it means. They may even wish to record it in their personal word dictionaries. As new words are added, old words and their illustrations can be compiled into a class Center Stage Words dictionary.

A variation on the idea above comes from Beck, McKeown, and Kucan (2002). The authors suggest making a target-words bulletin board. Choose a book you've read to your students and directly taught words from. Place the cover of the book (or a photocopy of it) on the board. Then write up to three new vocabulary words from that book on index cards, one word per card, and attach them next to the cover. (Choose no more than three words from any given story.) This strategy will help you remember to refer to the words when you and your students come across them in other situations throughout the day. It also keeps your students focused on the chosen words, so they recognize them in other contexts. You can place more than one book cover and set of words on the board if you wish.

The Real McCoy

Look around your home or visit a dollar store for common objects that your students may not be able to identify and bring as many examples as possible to school. Display them prominently and take time to discuss them when appropriate. Your best bet for helping students to develop and retain their listening and speaking vocabularies is to relate the items to your current unit of study in one of the content areas. Give students plenty of supervised opportunities to handle the objects and get them talking about them.

Here are some items you may want to consider.

Seashells for an ocean unit: conch, scallop, clam, mussel, crab, oyster

Tools for a unit on simple machines: hammer, screwdriver, pliers, wrench, drill, level

Socks: dress, running, wool, argyle, knee, athletic

Kitchen gadgets for simple machines or nutrition study: spatula, whisk, colander, garlic press

Art: watercolors, portrait, collages, Cray-Pas

Balls for a study of properties: tennis, baseball, football, basketball, ping pong, golf, whiffle

When you introduce these objects, give their appropriate names and discuss each item's purpose, using descriptive adjectives and strong verbs—a great way to build everyday vocabularies. You can play a simplified version of Twenty Questions with these objects too. Children will ask you questions until they figure out which tool, gadget, or seashell you are thinking of, for example, and will need to use lots of specific words in the process!

Bibliography

Baumann, J. and E. Kame'enui, eds. (2004). *Vocabulary Instruction: Research to Practice*. New York: Guilford.

Beck, I., M. McKeown, and L. Kucan. (2002). *Bringing Words to Life: Robust Vocabulary Instruction*. New York: Guilford.

Blachowicz, C. and P. Fisher. (2006). *Teaching Vocabulary in All Classrooms*. Columbus, OH: Pearson.

Guglielmino, L. M. (1986) The Affective Edge: Using Songs and Music in ESL Instruction. *Adult Literacy and Basic Education*, 10, 19-26.

Jensen, E. (2004). *Brain Compatible Strategies*. Thousand Oaks, CA: Corwin Press.

National Institute of Child Health and Human Development, NIH, DHHS. (2000). Report of the National Reading Panel: Teaching Children to Read (00-4769). Washington, DC: U.S. Government Printing Office.

Paynter, D., E. Bodrova, and J. Doty. (2005). *For the Love of Words: Vocabulary Instruction that Works*. San Francisco: Jossey-Bass.

Rog, L. (2001). *Early Literacy Instruction in Kindergarten*. Newark, DE: International Reading Association.

Trelease, Jim. (2001). *The Read-Aloud Handbook*. New York: Penguin.

Reproducibles

WONDERFUL WORDS TO USE WHEN I WRITE

Name:

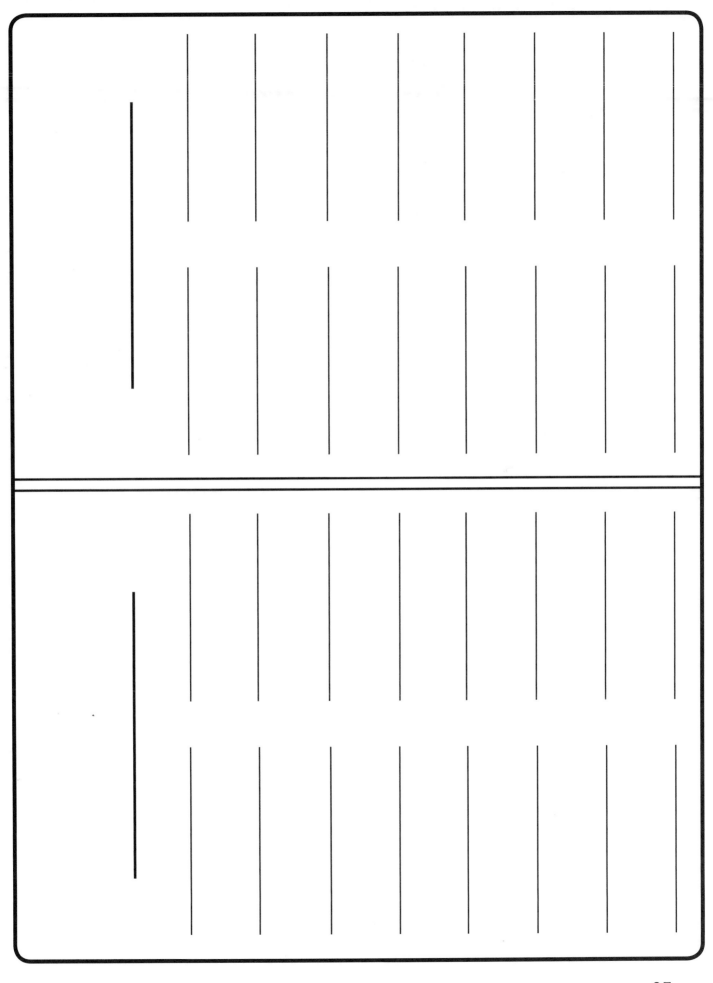

65

My Personal Pocket Thesaurus

Name:

Other ways I can say

_____

Other ways I can say

_____

67

cubbies	exit
basket	chart
faucet	carpet
easel	art supplies
keyboard	windowpane
chalk ledge	cinder blocks
monitor	blinds
closet	speaker

intercom	table
floor tile	paper
door hinge	blocks
screen	books
switch	clock
outlet	window
door	chair
desk	phone

69

glue	rug
scissors	hook
markers	counters
crayons	shelf
pencils	computer
light	stapler
tape	board
wall	games

71

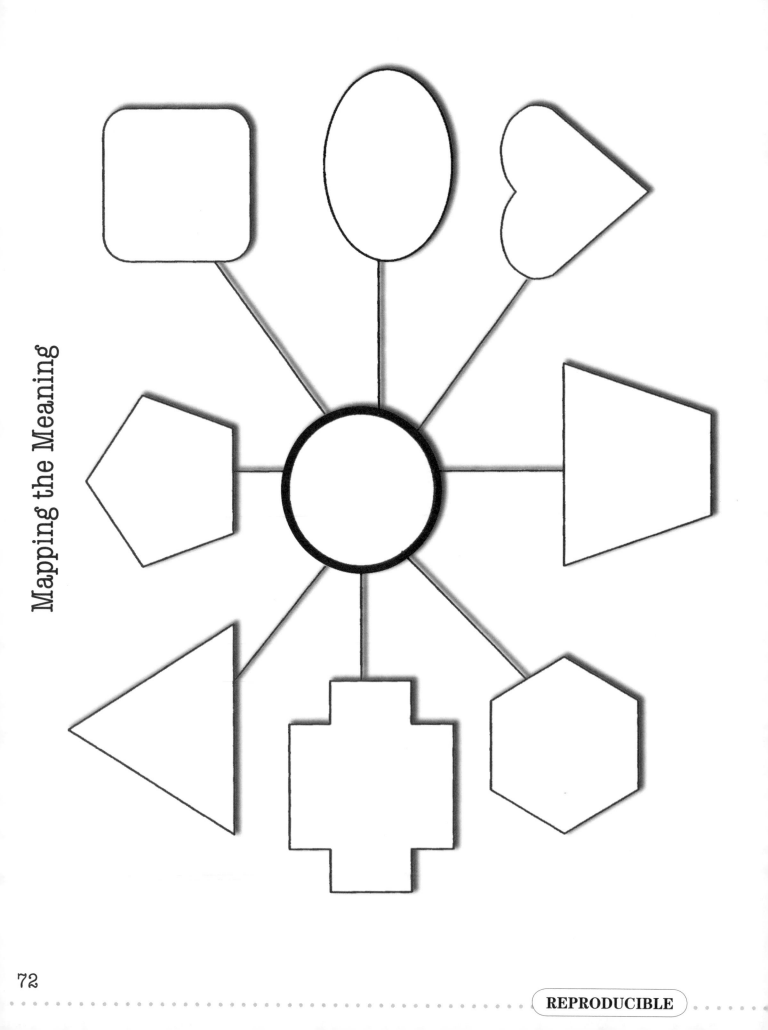

Mapping the Meaning

72

Concept Dictionary

73

Round Robin Senses

	Familiar	Different
Sight		
Smell		
Taste		
Hearing		
Touch		

Keep Your Ears Open

Name _____   **Week of** _____

Words I heard . . .	on TV	on the computer	in a video game	in a book somebody read to me	my parents say	in a movie	in a store or restaurant

Talk It Out

Name _____   Category _____

Index

Note: Page numbers in *italics* indicate reproducibles to be used with activities.

INDEX

Bring author, presenter, and former teacher Laureen Reynolds to your school for on-site training.

To learn how, call (877) 388-2054.